I0814078

HISTORY OF PIRATES

KENNY ABDO

Fly!
An Imprint of Abdo Zoom
abdobooks.com

abdobooks.com

Published by Abdo Zoom, a division of ABDO, P.O. Box 398166, Minneapolis, Minnesota 55439.

Printed in the United States of America, North Mankato, Minnesota.
102021
012022

Photo Credits: Alamy, Everett Collection, Getty Images, Granger Collection, iStock, Shutterstock
Production Contributors: Kenny Abdo, Jennie Forsberg, Grace Hansen
Design Contributors: Candice Keimig, Neil Klinepier, Laura Graphenteen

Library of Congress Control Number: 2021940197

Publisher's Cataloging-in-Publication Data

Names: Abdo, Kenny, author.
Title: History of pirates / by Kenny Abdo
Description: Minneapolis, Minnesota : Abdo Zoom, 2022 | Series: Pirates | Includes online resources and index.
Identifiers: ISBN 9781098226855 (lib. bdg.) | ISBN 9781644947005 (pbk.) | ISBN 9781098227692 (ebook) | ISBN 9781098228118 (Read-to-Me ebook)
Subjects: LCSH: Pirates--Juvenile literature. | Pirates--History--Juvenile literature. | Piracy--Juvenile literature.
Classification: DDC 910.4--dc23

HISTORY OF PIRATES

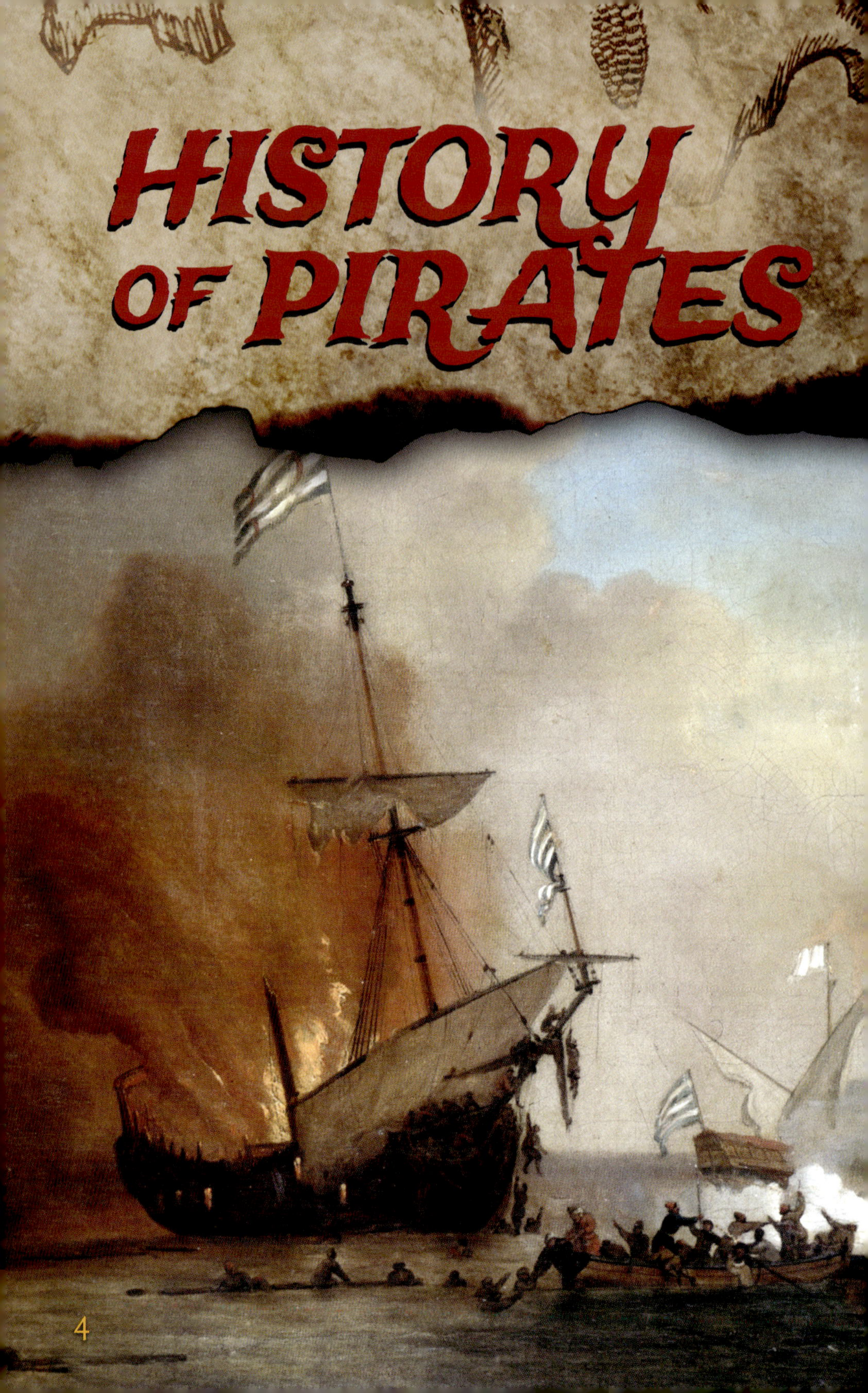

For centuries, pirates have seized many ships and the fascinations of historians!

The history of pirates is as exciting and mysterious as a well-worn treasure map used for navigating the open seas!

YE OLDE YARN

The word "pirate" comes from an old Greek word meaning "attempt." This led to the word peiratēs, which refers to a member of a group of robbers.

Pirates targeted popular shipping routes, like the English Channel. These paths would be lined with ships full of treasures for the taking.

Pirates followed a set of rules known as the **Pirate Code**. The laws would differ from one ship to another. A common rule in the Pirate Code was no fighting among **mates** onboard a ship.

VAST BOUNTY

More than 2,000 years ago, pirates in ancient Greece started targeting trading routes. They stopped any ship that passed by and cruelly robbed it.

Vikings were the most famous pirates in **medieval** Europe. Between the 8th and 12th centuries, they looted ships off the coasts of Western Europe and North Africa, and in the Baltic Sea.

The **Spanish Main** was a popular target in the 16th century. Spanish ships used it to carry treasure to Europe. These were the ships pirates dreamed of.

Piracy peaked between the 1650s and 1730s. This was known as the **Golden Age of Piracy**. During this time, there were many types of pirates that operated in different places, like the Mediterranean and Caribbean.

At the turn of the 18th century, an earthquake destroyed a major Caribbean **port**. So, pirates there moved on to explore other places like Rhode Island and Bermuda.

Pirates were supported by countries, known as pirate states, along the **Barbary Coast**. In the early 1800s the British, French, and U.S. navies ended piracy in this area.

BARBARY STATES
English Miles
100
0
100
200
MEDITERRANEAN SEA
SARDINIA
Cagliari
G. of Cagliari
Minorca
Mahon
Islands
Ustica I.
Palermo
Trapani
Ægades Is.
Marsala
Mazzara
SICILY
Girgenti
Licata
Pantellaria
Malta
Gozo
Valetta
(British)
Linosa
Bay of Tunis
Bizerta
Tunis
Goletta
Kelibia
Nabeul
Hammamet
Gulf of Hammamet
Susa
Monastir
Mahadia
Ras Kapudia
Kairwan
Bedja
Zaghuan
Kef
Constantine
Philippeville
Bona
Collo
Jijelli
Bougie
Batna
Lambese
Biskra
Tebessa
Gafsa
Kasrin
TUNIS
Sfax
Karkena Is.
Gulf of Cabes
Jerba I.
Cabes
Shott Jerid
Nefta
El Wad
Tugurt
Wargla
Ghardaia
Metlili
El Golea
Sahara
Region of Sand Hills
Tinghard
Hammada el Homra
Ghadames
TRIPOLI
Tripoli
Jefara Plain
Jeb. Nefusa
El Homra
Bir Nasra
Gharia
Temassanin
El Biodh
Bu Sada
Boghar
Aumale
8
12
4
36
32
28

Piracy slowed down around the 1900s. Modern pirate attacks still happen off the coast of Somalia and in the South China Sea. Instead of large ships, these pirates use small speedboats.

Pirates have terrorized the **briny deep** for thousands of years. Proving that they won't be walking the plank anytime soon.

GLOSSARY

Barbary Coast – the Mediterranean coast of northern Africa.

briny deep – another name for the ocean.

Golden Age of Piracy – a period between the 1650s and the 1730s when piracy was rampant in the Caribbean, the United Kingdom, the Indian Ocean, North America, and West Africa.

mates – a fellow member of a ship's crew.

medieval – a period in European history from about 500 to 1500 CE.

Pirate Code – rules pirate crews drafted up per ship. It included laws about how pirates were paid, healthcare, and what would happen if the code was broken.

port – a place where ships load or drop off goods.

Spanish Main – the mainland from Mexico, Peru, to the Caribbean.

ONLINE RESOURCES

To learn more about history of pirates, please visit **abdobooklinks.com** or scan this QR code. These links are routinely monitored and updated to provide the most current information available.

INDEX